Gisèle Freund

Gisèle Freund

The Poetry of the Portrait

Photographs of Writers and Artists

With a Preface by Gisèle Freund

SCHIRMER ART BOOKS

The preface by Gisèle Freund was translated from the French by John M. King.
The English edition was edited by Roger W. Benner.

SchirmerArt Books is an imprint of Schirmer/Mosel Verlag GmbH, Munich.
For trade information please contact:
Schirmer Art Books, John Rule, 40 Voltaire Rd., London SW4 6DH, England, or
Schirmer/Mosel Verlag, P.O. Box 401723, 80717 Munich, Germany

Typesetter: Typograph, Munich
Printing and binding: EBS, Verona

ISBN 3-88814-890-1
A Schirmer/Mosel Production

Program information via the Internet:
http://www.schirmer/mosel.de

In this little volume I have compiled a collection of about forty portraits of writers and artists it was my privilege to become acquainted with. I have often been asked: "How did you manage to meet and photograph so many famous writers and artists?" The answer is quite simple: "During the period when I photographed them they were only known to a small public. It wasn't until decades later that their works became famous and well known all over the world."

The majority of creative people are reluctant to have themselves photographed. Mostly sensitive and anxious, they feel they will survive more because of their works than because of any portrayal of their physical form, which temporarily harbored their anxiety.

Once we have enjoyed the ideas expressed in a book, we want to see the face behind them. This is the reason why publishers often print a picture of the author on the back of a book. The author is intent and anxious to create the best possible impression, for his or her portrait is the only corporeal contact with the reader.

None of us see ourselves as we are seen by others. We inhabit our face without seeing it, but we expose this part of the body to the first person who crosses our path in the street. We look at ourselves in the mirror, but it reflects our features the other way round. What is more, the pressures and proprieties of society have obliged us to wear a mask to conceal our emotions, our weariness and our disappointments. This is why the candid faces of children move us with their innocence.

When we see ourselves, we see not only our features but also our character, for the portrait we create of ourselves is of a psychological rather than a visual dimension. This explains why we rarely recognize ourselves in a photograph. For the writer whose only relationship with the reader is his or her portrait, the latter is of vital importance.

It is rare that those who are photographed are pleased with the result. This is one of the reasons why I did not make "portraits" my profession and why I have never owned a photography studio. I photographed nearly all the writers in their own homes, in the atmosphere they were familiar with. When they posed for me, I was fascinated by the faces of these creative people.

In my youth I was especially influenced by the realist movement, primarily reflected in the works of American writers. For photography it meant absolutely no retouching. I then lived in a minute attic studio. A spiral staircase led up to a very large terrace with a magnificent view of Paris. It was on this terrace that I took the first portrait of a writer: André Malraux.

At that time I was still a student, having chosen sociology and the history of art as the subjects of my thesis, and had taken up photography as a means of earning a little money to pay my way as a student. My parents were unable to help me, as the Nazi regime forbade money to be sent out of the country.

Malraux was only thirty-four at the time. We were friends, and when his book *La Condition humaine*, which was awarded the Prix Goncourt, was reprinted, his publisher Gaston Gallimard asked him for a portrait. So Malraux asked me to photograph him, knowing that I had recently started to earn my living as a photographer.

Very soon, I realized that in order to take a natural portrait it was necessary to use every means possible to prevent the subject from paying any attention to my little camera – a Leica and my companion all

my life, originally a present from my father for passing my *baccalauréat.*
The main thing men, writers in particular, are interested in is their
work. As I had previously read the works of people I photographed,
I was able to strike up a conversation about what they had written.
The result was that they soon forgot my camera. This little trick
helped me to take natural photos, without any posing. I should add
that I was fascinated by writing.

I am indebted to two people from the world of literature who made it
possible for me to take my first portraits. Jean Paulhan was for over
thirty years the *éminence grise* of French literature. He was the director
of *La Nouvelle Revue Française*, published by éditions Gallimard. When I
arrived in France in 1933, I was introduced to him and he invited me
to come to his enormous office on Wednesday afternoons, the time
fixed for receiving visits from writers. In this way I met most writers of
the period.

The other person to whom I owe the privilege of becoming
acquainted with the writings of the avant-garde is Adrienne Monnier.
She had a little bookstore in the rue de l'Odéon and was renowned
among writers, her friends, for her infallible literary judgement. She
discovered almost all the writers, renowned nowadays but almost
unknown back then. Thanks to her kindness, I first read the works
of those she had discovered and it was also thanks to her that many
closed doors were opened to me, when I thought of photographing
the writers in color.

It was not until the end of 1938 that it was possible to buy 35mm
Kodachrome and Agfacolor films in France. Nowadays, millions of
photography enthusiasts use these films, but during the period before

World War II, they were not yet widely known. Color film had been invented long before, but it was not until now that the photography fan could actually use it. Professional photographers hardly ever used color because virtually no newspaper or magazine in France had the machines to print it. When I told Adrienne that I would like to photograph her friends in color, she, taking a passionate interest in everything that was new, offered to help me in this new venture.

The only color publications were printed in America and so it came about that she asked me to work for the publishers there. Consequently, one of the first writers I photographed in color for *Time* magazine was James Joyce who in 1939 published his last book, *Finnegans Wake.* This is the reason why I decided to put his picture on the cover of this little book.

It is not easy to take a portrait that reflects more than the outward appearance of a personality. It is easier to photograph artists, who know, by way of their trade, how to pose, but writers are somewhat reluctant. The friendships that grew between us helped them to confide in me. The understanding they showed me was an enormous help in the arduous task of presenting an authentic picture of themselves, more conform to the intimate reality of a creative person.

The endlessly long procession of faces that have marched before my eyes and that I will never see again has shown me that no two physiognomies are alike and that each face means a new discovery.

Plates

Walter Benjamin

1892 (Berlin) – 1940 (Port Bou, Spain)

Writer; emigrated to Paris in 1933

I Walter Benjamin, Paris, 1938

André Gide

1869 (Paris) – 1951 (Paris)

Writer, co-founder of *La Nouvelle Revue Française*;

Nobel Prize for Literature, 1947

2 André Gide, sitting beneath the death mask of Leopardi in his
apartment in rue Vanneau, Paris, 1939

Paul Valéry
1871 (Sète, France) – 1945 (Paris)
Writer and lyricist

3 Paul Valéry in his study, Paris, 1938

Adrienne Monnier
1892 (Paris) – 1955 (Paris)
Owner of the "La Maison des Amis des Livres" bookstore
in Paris, publisher, expert on modern French literature

4   Adrienne Monnier, Paris, 1938

5 Editorial meeting of the *Mesures* staff in Ville d'Avray, 1937
From left to right: Sylvia Beach, Mrs. Church, Vladimir Nabokov
(standing), Adrienne Monnier, Mme Paulhan, Henry Church, Henri
Michaux, Jean Paulhan (standing), Michel Leiris

Colette
1873 (Saint-Sauveur-en-Puisage, France) – 1954 (Paris)
Writer

6 Colette, Paris, 1939

7 James Joyce with Adrienne Monnier and Sylvia Beach, who issued
Ulysses, at the "Shakespeare & Co." bookstore, Paris, 1938

James Joyce
1882 (Dublin, Ireland) – 1941 (Zurich, Switzerland)
Writer

8 The hands of James Joyce, Paris, 1938

9 James Joyce with magnifying glass, Paris, 1939

George Bernard Shaw
1856 (Dublin, Ireland) – 1950 (Ayot St. Lawrence, England)
Writer and dramatist; Nobel Prize for Literature, 1925

10 George Bernard Shaw in the moonlight, London, 1939

Virginia Woolf
1882 (London) – 1941 (River Ouse, near Newhaven, England)
Writer

11 Virgina Woolf at her home in London, 1939

T. S. Eliot
1888 (St. Louis, Missouri) – 1965 (London)
Poet and critic; settled in London in 1914;
Nobel Prize for Literature, 1948

12 T. S. Eliot, Paris, 1939

Jean Cocteau

1889 (Maisons-Laffitte, France) – 1963 (Milly-la-Fôret, France)

Poet, writer, dramatist, screenwriter, and director

13 Jean Cocteau in his apartment, sitting next to a glovemaker's sign, Paris, 1939

André Breton
1896 (Tinchebray, France) – 1968 (Paris)
Writer and main theorist of literary Surrealism

14 André Breton at the flea market, Paris, 1957

Louis Aragon
1897 (Paris) – 1982 (Paris)
Writer and Surrealist

15 Louis Aragon, Paris, 1939

Elsa Triolet
1896 (Moscow) – 1970 (Saint-Arnoult-en-Yvelines, France)
Writer, essayist

16 Elsa Triolet, Paris, 1939

André Malraux
1901 (Paris) – 1976 (Creteil, near Paris)
Writer and politician

17 André Malraux, Paris, 1935

Jean-Paul Sartre
1905 (Paris) – 1980 (Paris)
Philosopher and writer;
Nobel Prize for Literature, 1964

18 Jean-Paul Sartre, Paris, 1939

Simone de Beauvoir

1908 (Paris) – 1986 (Paris)

Writer, essayist

19   Simone de Beauvoir the day she was awarded the Prix Goncourt,
Paris, 1952

20 Simone de Beauvoir, Paris, 1952

Jean Paulhan
1884 (Nîmes, France) – 1968 (Boissise-la-Bertrand, France)
Writer, director of *La Nouvelle Revue Française* and editor
of the *Nouvelle N.R.F.*

21 Jean Paulhan, Paris, 1947

Peggy Guggenheim
1898 (New York City) – 1979 (near Venice, Italy)
Art collector, museum founder

Herbert Read
1893 (Kirbymoorside, England) – 1968 (Malton, England)
Writer, lyricist, essayist, art critic

22 Peggy Guggenheim and Herbert Read, Paris, 1939

Henri Matisse

1869 (Le Cateau, France) – 1956 (Nice, France)

Painter and graphic artist

23 Henri Matisse, Paris, 1948

Pierre Bonnard

1867 (Fontenay-aux-Roses, France) – 1947 (Le Cannet, near Cannes)

Painter and graphic artist

24 Pierre Bonnard, Le Cannet, 1946

Marcel Duchamp

1887 (Blainville, near Rouen, France) – 1968 (Neuilly, France)

Painter, object artist, founder of the Dada movement in New York

25 Marcel Duchamp, Paris, 1939

Le Corbusier

1887 (La Chaux-de-Fonds, Switzerland) – 1965 (Cap-Martin, France)

Architect and city planner

26 Le Corbusier, Paris, 1961

Henry Miller
1891 (New York City) – 1980 (Pacific Palisades, California)
Writer

27 Henry Miller, Paris, 1961

John Steinbeck
1902 (Salinas, California) – 1968 (New York City)
Writer; Nobel Prize for Literature, 1962

28 John Steinbeck, Paris, 1961

Samuel Beckett
1906 (Foxrock, Ireland) – 1989 (Paris)
Writer and dramatist; settled in Paris in 1936;
Nobel Prize for Literature, 1969

29 Samuel Beckett, Paris, 1964

Hermann Hesse
1877 (Calw, Germany) – 1962 (Montagnola, Switzerland)
Writer; settled in Switzerland in 1919;
Nobel Prize for Literature, 1946

30 Hermann Hesse in Montagnola, Switzerland, 1962

Paul Celan
1920 (Chernovtsy, Ukraine, formerly Romania) – 1970 (Paris)
Lyricist; settled in Paris in 1948

31 Paul Celan, Paris, 1970

Arthur Koestler
1905 (Budapest) – 1983 (London)
Writer; settled in England in 1940

32 Arthur Koestler, London, 1967

Julio Cortazar
1914 (Brussels) – 1984 (Paris)
Argentinean writer; settled in Paris in 1951

33 Julio Cortazar, Paris 1966

Pablo Neruda
1904 (Parral, Chile) – 1973 (Santiago de Chile)
Lyricist; Nobel Prize for Literature, 1971

34 Pablo Neruda, Santiago de Chile 1944

Diego Rivera
1886 (Guanajuato, Mexico) – 1957 (Mexico City)
Painter, especially of murals

35 Diego Rivera standing in front of his fresco *The Creation of the World*,
Mexico City, 1952

Frida Kahlo
1907 (Coyoacán, Mexico City) – 1954 (Mexico City)
Painter

36 Frida Kahlo, Mexico City, 1952

Jorge Luis Borges
1899 (Buenos Aires, Argentina) – 1986 (Geneva, Switzerland)
Writer and lyricist

37 Jorge Luis Borges, London, 1971

Ivan Illich
born 1926 (Vienna)
Critic of society and culture, humanitarian

38 Ivan Illich, Cuernavaca, Mexico, 1974

Aleksandr Solzhenitsyn
born 1918 (Kislovodsk, Russia)
Writer; Nobel Prize for Literature, 1970

39 Aleksandr Solzhenitsyn, Paris, 1975

Marguerite Yourcenar
1903 (Brussels) – 1987 (Northeast Harbor, Maine)
Writer; settled in USA in 1973; first woman to become
a member of the Académie française (1980)

40 Marguerite Yourcenar, Desert Island, Maine, 1976

Biographical Notes

1908   Gisèle Freund is born on December 19 in Berlin-Schöneberg.

1931   Study of Sociology and Art History in Freiburg and Frankfurt am Main under Theodor W. Adorno, Karl Mannheim, Norbert Elias, et al.

1933   Opposition against Hitler's regime. She avoids arrest by fleeing to Paris on May 30. She continues her studies at the Sorbonne.

1936   Her doctoral thesis on photography in France in the 19th century is printed by Adrienne Monnier. Freund is awarded French citizenship. In the fall of 1938, she becomes the first woman photographer in France to use 35mm color film for her portraits of writers and artists. First photo documentaries for *Vu*, *Weekly Illustrated*, and *Life*. Marriage.

1940   She flees occupied Paris to the Departement Lot in southern France, where she lives underground.

1942   Departure for Argentina at the invitation of Victoria Ocampo, director of the periodical *Sur* in Buenos Aires. Freund continues to work as a journalist and photographer and is cultural attaché for the Ministry of Information of Free France while in South America.

1945   She founds the "Ediciones Victoria" in Buenos Aires, which is intended to focus on publishing books about France.

1946   Return to Paris with three tons of food collected for writers and journalists, as well as a photo exhibition on art and culture in South America. This same year, Freund returns to South America as an emissary of the Musée de l'Homme and the Ministry of Information. Travels to Patagonia and Tierra del Fuego and returns with photographs and a film documentary.

1947   Joins the photo agency Magnum shortly after its founding. Travels to the USA, Canada, and Central and South America. Freund lectures there on contemporary literature, using her portraits of writers as illustrations.

1950   *Life* publishes her report on Evita Perón. Freund spends two years in Mexico. Friendship with painters Diego Rivera and Frida Kahlo.

1953   Return to Paris, now her permanent home.

1954   She breaks with Magnum. The FBI declares Freund an undesired; a planned reportage on the USA has to be called off.

1963   First joint exhibition in the Federal Republic of Germany: "The French Portrait in the 20th Century."

1965   Her book *James Joyce in Paris: His Final Years* is published in New York.

1968   Important exhibition at the Musée d'art moderne de la ville de Paris.

1970   Travels to Japan and the Middle East. Her autobiography *Le monde et ma caméra* is published in French and English.

1970-76   Travels in Europe, the USA, and Mexico.

1977   Freund is named president of the French association of photographers. First retrospective exhibition in the Federal Republic of Germany (Rheinisches Landesmuseum, Bonn). She participates in "documenta 6" in Kassel.

1978   In Germany, she is awarded the cultural prize of the Deutsche Gesellschaft für Kultur.

1980   In France, she receives the Grand Prix National des Arts for photography. Freund becomes a member of the National Foundation for Photography.

1981   She is commissioned to take the official portrait of François Mitterrand.

1982   Officier des Arts et Lettres.

1983   Chevalier de la Légion d'Honneur.

1986   Exhibition at the Galerie de France, Paris.

1987   Officier du Mérite.

1987-88   Academic year in the USA at the invitation of the Getty Foundation.

1988   Retrospective exhibition in the Werkbund-Archiv, Berlin.

1989   Dr. honoris causa of Bradford University, England.

1991   Large retrospective exhibition in Paris at the Musée national d'art moderne and publishing of the *Catalogue de l'œuvre photographique Gisèle Freund.*

Selected Bibliography

Books by Gisèle Freund

La Photographie en France au 19ème siècle, Paris, 1936
Mexique précolombien, Neuchâtel 1954 (German edition Munich, 1956)
James Joyce in Paris: His Final Years, New York, 1965
Photographie und bürgerliche Gesellschaft, Munich, 1968
Photographie und Gesellschaft, Munich, 1976
Memoiren des Auges, Frankfurt am Main, 1977
Fotografien 1932–1977. Exhibition catalogue, Rheinisches Landesmuseum, Bonn.
    With an essay by Klaus Honnef, Bonn, 1977
Drei Tage mit James Joyce, Frankfurt am Main, 1983
Photographien. With autobiographical essays and a preface by Christian Caujolle,
    Munich, 1985 (English edition, *Gisèle Freund: Photographer*, New York, 1985)
Gisèle Freund. Exhibition catalogue Werkbund-Archiv, Berlin, 1988
Gisèle Freund. Portrait, Paris, 1991 (German edition, *Gisèle Freund – Gespräche mit Rauda
    Jamis*, Munich, 1993)
Gisèle Freund. Die Frau mit der Kamera. Fotografien 1929–1988. Exhibition catalogue
    B·A·T KunstFoyer, Hamburg, 1992

Magazine Articles and Essays

Camera, Switzerland, November 1968
ICP Encyclopedia of Photography, International Center of Photography, New York,
    Autumn 1984
Kramer, Hilton, "The World in Gisèle Freund's Lens," *The New York Times*,
    December 28, 1979
Lehmann-Haupt, Christopher, "Books of the Times," *The New York Times*, July 2,
    1980
Monnier, Adrienne, "In the Land of Faces," *Verve*, Paris, Nos. 5-6, 1939
Witkin, Lee, and Barbara London, *The Photography Collector's Guide*, Boston, New York
    Graphic Society, 1979

Index of Persons
(Numerals refer to the plates)